Hot Math Topics

Problem Solving, Communication, and Reasoning

Measurement and Geometry

grade
4

Carole Greenes
Linda Schulman Dacey
Rika Spungin

Dale Seymour Publications®
Parsippany, New Jersey

Acknowledgement: The authors wish to acknowledge the outstanding contributions of Mali Apple in the production of the *Hot Math Topics* series. She has given careful attention to the content, design, and art, and helped shepherd the program through from its inception to its completion. Thank you, Mali.

Dale Seymour Publications
an imprint of Pearson Learning
299 Jefferson Road
Parsippany, New Jersey 07054-0480
www.pearsonlearning.com
800-321-3106

Editorial Manager: Carolyn Coyle
Project Editor: Mali Apple
Production/Manufacturing Director: Janet Yearian
Production/Manufacturing Manager: Karen Edmonds
Production/Manufacturing Coordinator: Karen Mancinelli
Art Director: Jim O'Shea
Cover Design: Tracey Munz
Cover and Interior Illustrations: Jared Lee
Computer Graphics: Alan Noyes

ISBN 0-7690-0836-4

2 3 4 5 6 7 8 9 10-ML-09 08 07 06

This Book Is Printed
On Recycled Paper

contents

Introduction

Why Was *Hot Math Topics* Developed?

The *Hot Math Topics* series was developed for several reasons:

- to offer students practice and maintenance of previously learned skills and concepts
- to enhance problem solving and mathematical reasoning abilities
- to build literacy skills
- to nurture collaborative learning behaviors

Practicing and maintaining concepts and skills

Although textbooks and core curriculum materials do treat the topics explored in this series, their treatment is often limited by the lesson format and the page size. As a consequence, there are often not enough opportunities for students to practice newly acquired concepts and skills related to the topics, or to connect the topics to other content areas. *Hot Math Topics* provides the necessary practice and mathematical connections.

Similarly, core instructional programs often do not do a very good job of helping students maintain their skills. Although textbooks do include reviews of previously learned material, they are frequently limited to sidebars or boxed-off areas on one or two pages in each chapter, with four or five exercises in each box. Each set of problems is intended only as a sampling of previously taught topics, rather than as a complete review. In the selection and placement of the review exercises, little or no attention is given to levels of complexity of the problems. By contrast, *Hot Math Topics* targets specific topics and gives students more experience with concepts and skills related to them. The problems are sequenced by difficulty, allowing students to hone their skills. And, because they are not tied to specific lessons, the problems can be used at any time.

Enhancing problem solving and mathematical reasoning abilities

Hot Math Topics presents students with situations in which they may use a variety of problem solving strategies, including

- designing and conducting experiments to generate or collect data
- guessing, checking, and revising guesses
- organizing data in lists or tables in order to identify patterns and relationships
- choosing appropriate computational algorithms and deciding on a sequence of computations
- using inverse operations in "work backward" solution paths

For their solutions, students are also required to bring to bear various methods of reasoning, including

- deductive reasoning
- inductive reasoning
- proportional reasoning

For example, to solve clue-type problems, students must reason deductively and make inferences about mathematical relationships in order to generate candidates for the solutions and to hone in on those that meet all of the problem's conditions.

To identify and continue a pattern and then write a rule for finding the next term in that pattern, students must reason inductively.

To find actual length from scale drawings and to convert measurement units, students must reason proportionally.

To estimate or compare magnitudes of numbers, or to determine the type of number appropriate for a given situation, students must apply their number sense skills.

Building communication and literacy skills

Hot Math Topics offers students opportunities to write and talk about mathematical ideas. For many problems, students must describe their solution paths, justify their solutions, give their opinions, or write or tell stories.

Some problems have multiple solution methods. With these problems, students may have to compare their methods with those of their peers and talk about how their approaches are alike and different.

Other problems have multiple solutions, requiring students to confer to be sure they have found all possible answers.

Nurturing collaborative learning behaviors

Several of the problems can be solved by students working together. Some are designed specifically as partner problems. By working collaboratively, students can develop expertise in posing questions that call for clarification or verification, brainstorming solution strategies, and following another person's line of reasoning.

What Is in *Measurement and Geometry?*

This book contains 100 problems and tasks that focus on measurement and geometry. The mathematics content, the mathematical connections, the problem solving strategies, and the communication skills that are emphasized are described below.

Mathematics content

Measurement and geometry problems and tasks require students to

- use spatial reasoning
- identify, describe, and compare two-dimensional and three-dimensional figures
- explore transformations of plane figures
- identify lines of symmetry of plane figures
- compute and relate areas and perimeters of plane figures
- identify special angles
- compute and compare volumes of common three-dimensional figures
- compute with and convert among metric units of measure and among customary units of measure
- use number sense and measurement sense
- estimate, make, and use measurements
- interpret scatter plots, coordinate graphs, and scale drawings

Mathematical connections

In these problems and tasks, connections are made to these other topic areas:

- arithmetic
- algebra
- graphs
- statistics

Problem solving strategies

Measurement and Geometry problems and tasks offer students opportunities to use one or more of several problem solving strategies.

- **Formulate Questions:** When data are presented in displays or text form, students must pose one or more questions that can be answered using the given data.

- **Complete Stories:** When confronted with an incomplete story, students must supply the missing information and then check that the story makes sense.

- **Organize Information:** To ensure that several solution candidates for a problem are considered, students may have to organize information by drawing a picture, making a list, or constructing a chart.

- **Guess, Check, and Revise:** In some problems, students have to identify or generate candidates for the solution and then check whether those candidates match the conditions of the problem. If the conditions are not satisfied, other possible solutions must be generated and verified.

- **Identify and Continue Patterns:** To identify the next term or terms in a sequence, students have to recognize the relationship between successive terms and then generalize that relationship.

- **Use Logic:** Students have to reason deductively, from clues, to make inferences about the solution to a problem. They must reason proportionally to determine which of two buys is better. They have to reason inductively to continue geometric patterns. They have to reason spatially to view constructions from various perspectives.

- **Work Backward:** In some problems, the output is given and students must determine the input by identifying mathematical relationships between the input and output and applying inverse operations.

Communication skills

Problems and tasks in *Measurement and Geometry* are designed to stimulate communication. As part of the solution process, students may have to

- describe their thinking steps
- describe patterns and rules
- find alternate solution methods and solution paths
- identify other possible answers
- formulate problems for classmates to solve
- compare estimates, solutions, and methods with classmates
- make drawings to clarify mathematical relationships
- describe spatial relationships and define terms

These communication skills are enhanced when students interact with one another and with the teacher. By communicating both orally and in writing, students develop their understanding and use of the language of mathematics.

How Can *Hot Math Topics* Be Used?

The problems may be used as practice of newly learned concepts and skills, as maintenance of previously learned ideas, and as enrichment experiences for early finishers or more advanced students.

They may be used in class or assigned for homework. If used during class, they may be selected to complement lessons dealing with a specific topic or assigned every week as a means of keeping skills alive and well. Because the problems often require the application of various problem solving strategies and reasoning methods, they may also form the basis of whole-class lessons whose goals are to develop expertise with specific problem solving strategies or methods.

The problems, which are sequenced from least to most difficult, may be used by students working in pairs or on their own. The selection of problems may be made by the teacher or the students based on their needs or interests. If the plan is for students to choose problems, you may wish to copy individual problems onto card stock and laminate them, and establish a problem card file.

To facilitate record keeping, a Management Chart is provided on page 6. The chart can be duplicated so that there is one for each student. As a problem is completed, the space corresponding to that problem's number may be shaded. An Award Certificate is included on page 6 as well.

How Can Student Performance Be Assessed?

Measurement and Geometry problems and tasks provide you with opportunities to assess students'

- knowledge of measurement and geometry
- problem solving abilities
- mathematical reasoning methods
- communication skills

Observations

Keeping anecdotal records helps you to remember important information you gain as you observe students at work. To make observations more manageable, limit each observation to a group of from four to six students or to one of the areas noted above. You may find that using index cards facilitates the recording process.

Discussions

Many of the *Measurement and Geometry* problems and tasks allow for multiple answers or may be solved in a variety of ways. This built-in richness motivates students to discuss their work with one another. Small groups or class discussions are appropriate. As students share their approaches to the problems, you will gain additional insights into their content knowledge, mathematical reasoning, and communication abilities.

Scoring responses

You may wish to holistically score students' responses to the problems and tasks. The simple scoring rubric below uses three levels: high, medium, and low.

High	Medium	Low
• Solution demonstrates that the student knows the concepts and skills.	• Solution demonstrates that the student has some knowledge of the concepts and skills.	• Solution shows that the student has little or no grasp of the concepts and skills.
• Solution is complete and thorough.	• Solution is complete.	• Solution is incomplete or contains major errors.
• Student communicates effectively.	• Student communicates somewhat clearly.	• Student does not communicate effectively.

Portfolios

Having students store their responses to the problems in *Hot Math Topics* portfolios allows them to see improvement in their work over time. You may want to have them choose examples of their best responses for inclusion in their permanent portfolios, accompanied by explanations as to why each was chosen.

Students and the assessment process

Involving students in the assessment process is central to the development of their abilities to reflect on their own work, to understand the assessment standards to which they are held accountable, and to take ownership for their own learning. Young children may find the reflective process difficult, but with your coaching, they can develop such skills.

Discussion may be needed to help students better understand your standards for performance. Ask students such questions as, "What does it mean to communicate *clearly*?" "What is a *complete* response?" Some students may want to use the high-medium-low rubric to score their responses.

Participation in peer-assessment tasks will also help students to better understand the performance standards. In pairs or small groups, students can review each other's responses and offer feedback. Opportunities to revise work may then be given.

What Additional Materials Are Needed?

Some manipulatives and measurement tools are required for solving the problems in *Measurement and Geometry:* dot paper, 5-by-5 dot grids, graph paper, large paper clips, straws, square tiles, customary and metric measurement tools for length, scissors, cubes, a mirror, and a calculator. If available, tangrams, and square geoboards with rubber bands, may be helpful for some students.

Management Chart

Name _____

When a problem or task is completed, shade the box with that number.

1	2	3	4	5	6	7	8	9	10
11	12	13	14	15	16	17	18	19	20
21	22	23	24	25	26	27	28	29	30
31	32	33	34	35	36	37	38	39	40
41	42	43	44	45	46	47	48	49	50
51	52	53	54	55	56	57	58	59	60
61	62	63	64	65	66	67	68	69	70
71	72	73	74	75	76	77	78	79	80
81	82	83	84	85	86	87	88	89	90
91	92	93	94	95	96	97	98	99	100

Award Certificate

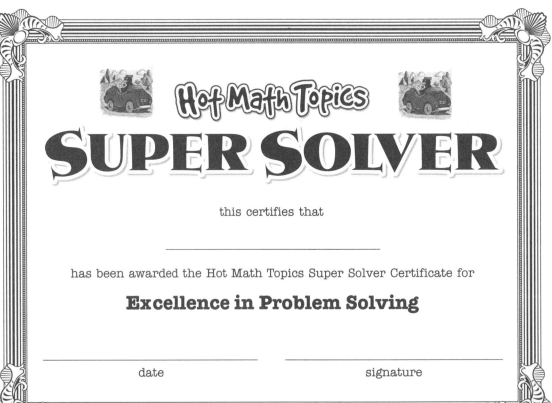

Hot Math Topics

SUPER SOLVER

this certifies that

_____

has been awarded the Hot Math Topics Super Solver Certificate for

Excellence in Problem Solving

_____   _____
date   signature

Problems
and Tasks

Connect the dots to make 3 squares.

● ● ●
● ● ●
● ●
●

Joy opened a half-gallon of milk.

She used the milk and 3 packages of mix to make pudding.

How much milk did she have left?

Erik, Carl, Huang, and Pedro are friends.

Write clue 3 so that the friends can be ordered by height.

Clues

1. Erik is taller than Huang and Pedro.

2. Carl is shorter than Erik but taller than Huang.

3. _____

Put the names in order.

_____ _____ _____ _____

Shortest   **Tallest**

- -

Conduct an experiment.

- Walk from your classroom to the principal's office.

- Count your walking steps.

- Now measure one of your steps.

- Calculate the distance to the principal's office to the nearest foot.

Compare your distance with the distance found by 3 classmates.

© Dale Seymour Publications®

Write two math story problems that use these facts.

- A kitchen sink holds about 10 gallons of water.
- A dollar bill is about 6 inches long.
- A doorway is about 1 yard wide.
- A cup holds 8 ounces of water.

Give your problems to a classmate to solve.

Gina, Kiran, and Kyle each made a polygon on a geoboard.

- Gina: "My polygon has some right angles."
- Kiran: "My polygon has 10 sides."
- Kyle: "My polygon is an octagon."

Match each student to a polygon.

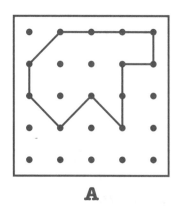

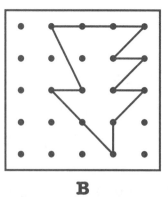

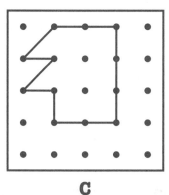

A   B   C

Put numbers on the lines.

Be sure the numbers fit the facts.

The temperature at the park was _____ °F at 8 A.M.

Two hours later, at _____ , the temperature was
_____ degrees warmer, or _____ °F.

Three hours later, at _____ P.M., the temperature
had risen to 73°F.

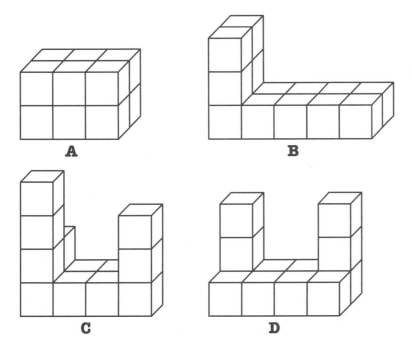

- -

Which two shapes have the same volume?

**Assume there are no cubes you can't see,
unless they are needed to hold up another cube.**

A

B

C

D

If you look at the part of each figure in front of the mirror together with its reflection, which will show a square?

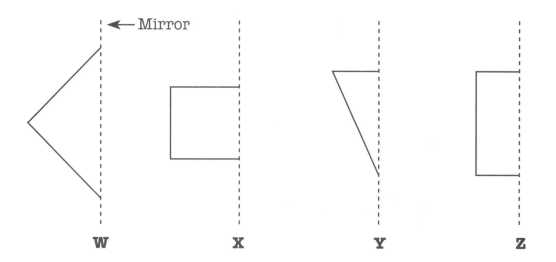

W   X   Y   Z

Score 3 points for a triangle and 4 points for a quadrilateral.

Use the letters.

Name the triangles.

Name the quadrilaterals.

What is the total score for this design?

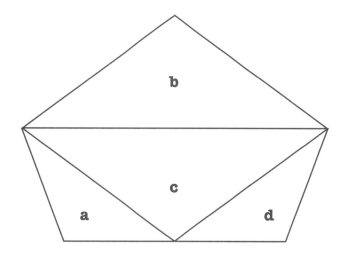

11

How many hours do you sleep each night?

Keep a log.

Record the number of hours you sleep each night for 7 nights.

Find the average number of hours.

Compare your average with the averages of your classmates.

- -

12

Fill in the story with the units of measurement that make sense.

Lucy is 10 _____ old.

Every day after school, she rides her bicycle a distance of 7 _____.

Her bicycle is 5 _____, or 60 _____, long.

It has wheels that are 22 _____ high.

After riding, Lucy drinks 8 _____ of water.

A bowling ball weighs 40 grams more than 5 kilograms.

What is the bowling ball's weight in grams?

- -

There are 20 pieces of chalk in a new box.

Each piece of chalk is 10 centimeters long.

If all the pieces of chalk are placed end to end, how many meters long would the line be?

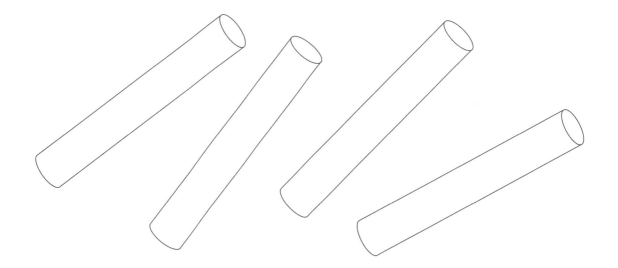

All of these are zeekles.

None of these are zeekles.

Which of these are zeekles? Why?

A　　**B**　　**C**　　**D**　　**E**

- -

How many weigh the same as 1 ?

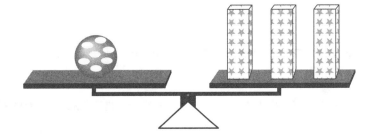

Draw the mirror image of A on B.

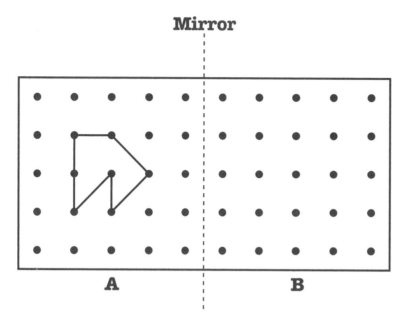

Assume your heart beats about 35 times in 30 seconds.

About how many times does your heart beat in 1 hour?

Use the thermometer to help you fill in the blanks.

The record high temperature for Boston on January 1 was set in 1890 and was _____ °F.

The record low temperature for Boston on January 1 was set in 1899 and was _____ °F.

The record high is _____ degrees higher than the temperature at which water freezes.

The record low is _____ degrees lower than the temperature at which water freezes.

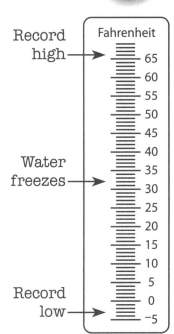

Tell how you can use the information on the sign to estimate the length of this line in millimeters:

_____

pyramid *triangular prism*

cylinder *rectangular prism*

Which shape am I?

- Two of my faces are triangles.
- My other three faces are rectangles.

- -

Write directions for drawing this design for someone who can't see it.

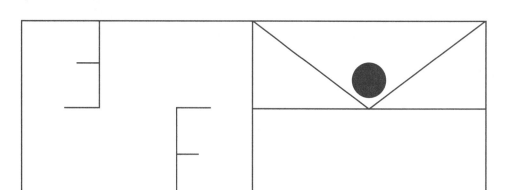

Have a classmate read your directions and draw the design.

Revise your directions if they aren't clear.

Use the clues to identify each family.

- There are 3 more children than bikes in the Rose family.

- There are 2 more bikes than children in the Saks family.

- In the Picó family, there are twice as many children as bikes.

- The Dells have a bike for each child.

A is the _____ family.

B is the _____ family.

C is the _____ family.

D is the _____ family.

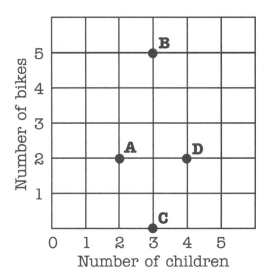

- -

You have these containers:

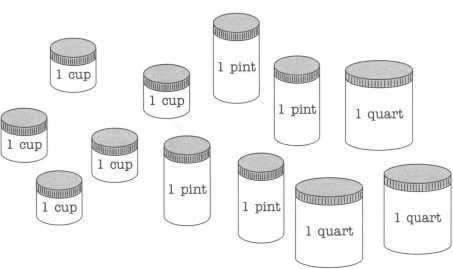

How many different ways can you use these containers to store 1 gallon of honey?

Make a list.

Tell 2 different ways to find the area of the polygon.

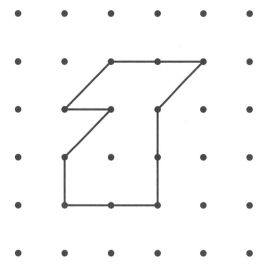

 = 1 square unit

In ancient times, a *fathom* was the length from fingertip to fingertip of outstretched arms.

1 fathom

Predict the length and width of your classroom in your fathoms.

Measure to check.

27

How is each of these solids different from the others?

A   B   C   D

28

A watercolor paintbrush is about 7 inches long and weighs about 1 ounce.

Imagine a line of paintbrushes as tall as you.

How much less than a pound would the paintbrushes weigh?

29

Which is the better buy?

Tell how you know.

- -

30

A quadrilateral has four sides.

List 2 other things you know about each of these quadrilaterals.

1. rectangle

2. parallelogram

3. rhombus

4. square

Compare your lists with a classmate's lists.

31

RIBBON SALE
50¢ a yard.
Sold only by the yard.

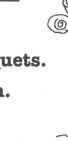

Mr. Silver is making bouquets.

He needs 40 feet of ribbon.

How much will it cost?

32

5280 feet equals
1 mile.

Mount Everest is on the border between Nepal
and Tibet.

At 29,028 feet high, it is the highest mountain in
the world.

About how many miles high is Mount Everest?

33

centimeters   liters   grams
meters   kilograms

Write in the units that make the best sense.

The height of a door is about 2 _____.

The mass of an apple is about 250 _____.

A fishbowl holds about 3 _____ of water.

The length of your thumb is about
4 _____.

The mass of a television set is about
27 _____.

- -

34

Work with a partner.

**Make a list of objects that are shaped like
a cylinder.**

35

Which has the greater perimeter? Tell how you know.

a pentagon with 4-inch sides

a hexagon with 4-inch sides

36

Are these claims reasonable? Explain your thinking.

- John drinks 2000 milliliters of water every day.

- John walked his neighbor's dog for 3 hours. He was paid with $1 bills that had a total mass of 1000 grams.

Make up three more claims.

Give them to a classmate to decide whether they are reasonable.

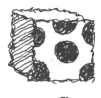 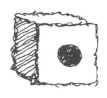

A **B** **C** **D**

What is the weight of A?

- A is 4 pounds heavier than B.
- B is 3 pounds lighter than C.
- C is twice as heavy as D.
- D weighs 2 pounds.

CHIPS
12 oz
$1.80

CHIPS
1 lb 8 oz
$3.10

Estimate.

Which size box of chips is the better buy?

Tell how you decided.

Get 24 cubes.

How many different rectangular prisms can you make using all 24 cubes?

Tell the dimensions of each prism.

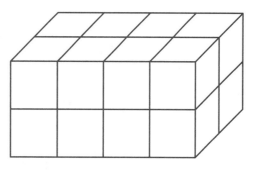

This rectangular prism is made of 16 cubes.

Which container holds the most water? How did you decide?

A   6 pints

B   24 ounces

C   ½ gallon

D   5 quarts

41

A square is 4 centimeters on a side.

How many different-size rectangles, with sides that are whole numbers of inches, have the same perimeter as the square?

Make a list.

Compare your list with a classmate's list.

- -

The table lists high temperatures for one day in February.

Use the map and what you know about geography to complete the table.

List the city for each temperature.

Tell how you decided.

42

High Temperatures

City	Temp.
	32°F
	45°F
	54°F
	71°F
	82°F

A 180-pound astronaut weighs about 30 pounds on the moon.

Mark weighs 90 pounds on Earth.

About how much would he weigh on the moon?

Tell how you decided.

- -

This is a net for a cube.

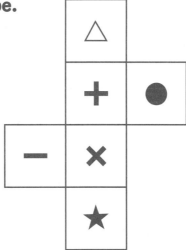

Which of these shows the cube when it is folded?

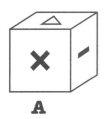   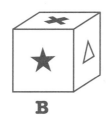   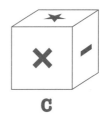   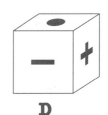

A   **B**   **C**   **D**

Find the shortest route from Flower City to Lyle.

Write directions for driving along that route.

Use highway numbers and distances in your directions.

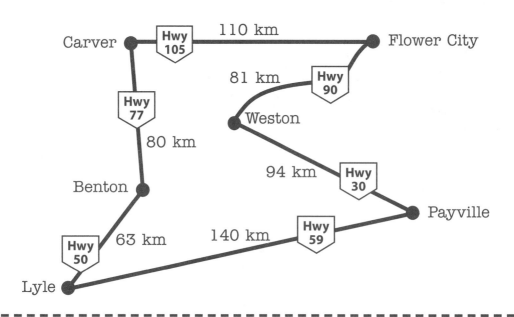

Use a calculator to help you.

What is your height in

- millimeters? _____
- centimeters? _____
- decimeters? _____
- meters? _____

Give measurements to the nearest whole number.

The area of square ABCD is 64 square inches.

What is the area of the shaded section?

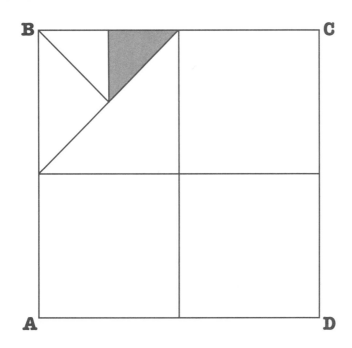

Think of a digital clock.

For how many minutes does at least one 9 show in the 12 hours from 8 A.M. until 8 P.M.?

How did you decide?

Four have a mass of 76 grams.

Six ⬤ have a mass of 36 grams.

How many grams on the right side will balance this scale?

List the steps you used to answer the question.

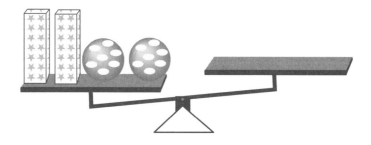

If you draw a line across a hexagon, you can make a quadrilateral and a hexagon.

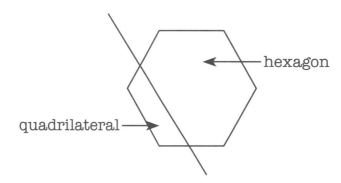

hexagon

quadrilateral

How many different pairs of polygons can you make by drawing a line across a hexagon?

Guess first. Then check by drawing.

List the pairs of polygons.

Compare your list with a classmate's list.

Write directions to tell a classmate how to make this building with 44 cubes.

Have a classmate follow your directions.

Check. Were your directions clear?

51

Here's what you do . . .

---

36 175 25 44 11

52

Fill in the blanks.

Use the numbers above.

The story must make sense.

Taking a bath uses about _____ gallons of water.

Taking a shower uses about _____ gallons of water.

A shower takes _____ fewer gallons, or _____ fewer quarts, of water than a bath.

Showering once a day for a week uses about _____ gallons of water.

Here are 2 copies of a figure made
with squares.

On copy 1, draw lines to separate
the figure into rectangles.

Find the area of each rectangle.

Find the area of the figure.

On copy 2, show a different way
of drawing lines to form
rectangles.

Find the area of the figure.

Are the areas of the two copies
the same?

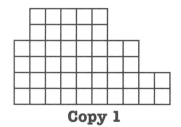

Copy 1

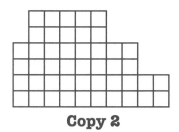

Copy 2

- -

Select five objects in
your classroom.

Estimate the length
of each object in
centimeters.

Then measure
each object.

Keep a record of
your estimates and
measurements.

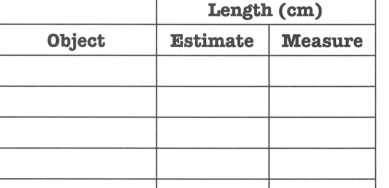

Object	Length (cm)	
	Estimate	Measure

Which of these can be folded to make a rectangular prism?

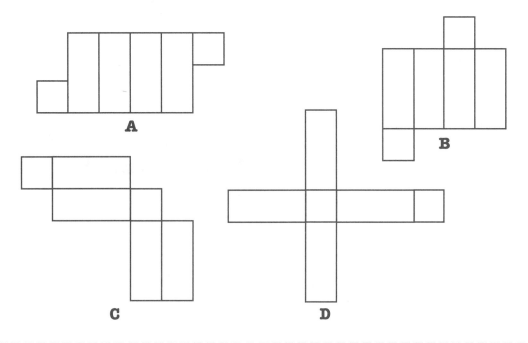

- -

A *diagonal* is a line segment that connects two vertices that are not next to each other.

A pentagon has 5 diagonals.

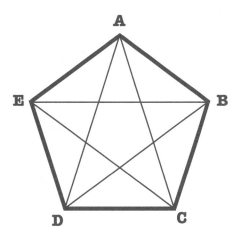

How many more diagonals does an octagon have than a square?

You want 5 pounds of weights.

You have these weights.

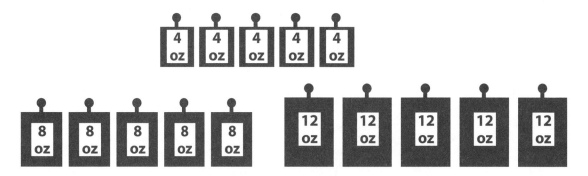

Choose the fewest number of weights possible that total 5 pounds.

List the weights and the number of each.

- -

A square has an area of 49 square feet.
A rectangle has an area of 24 square feet.
Its length is 2 feet longer than its width.
Which shape has the greater perimeter?
Tell how you know.

On dot paper, draw a square, a rectangle, and a triangle.

Give each shape an area of 4 square units.

59

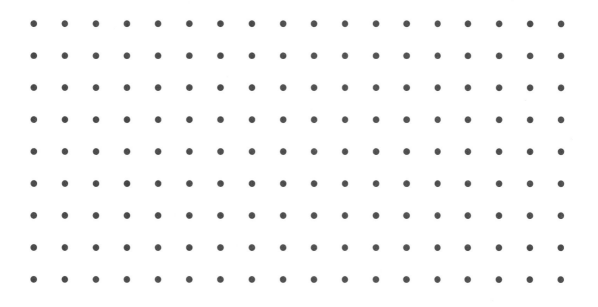

The diameter of a quarter is about 25 millimeters.

60

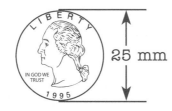

25 mm

What is the value of a line of quarters that is 40 meters long?

The pattern continues.

Describe the pattern.

What will be the volume of figure 4?

 = 1 cubic unit

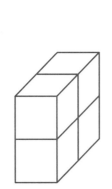

Figure 1

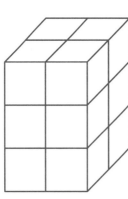

Figure 2

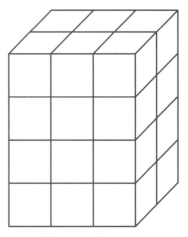

Figure 3

- -

Write the names under the chairs.

Give two answers that fit the facts.

- Carmen, Reva, Ken, Isaac, and Tracy are sitting in a row.

- Carmen is the only person between Reva and Ken.

- Reva is the only person between Carmen and Isaac.

- Tracy is sitting at the far right.

_____ _____ _____ _____ _____

_____ _____ _____ _____ _____

Micky and Elsa each used small cubes to build a bigger cube.

- Each face of Micky's cube is 5 cubes long.

- Each face of Elsa's cube is 7 cubes long.

How many more small cubes did Elsa use than Micky?

Get a tangram set, or trace and cut out this tangram pattern.

Using all 7 pieces, make 2 squares that are the same size.

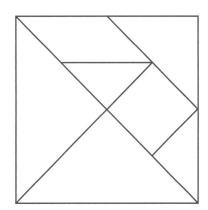

A mirror is placed upright on each mirror line.

Draw what you see when you look in the mirror.

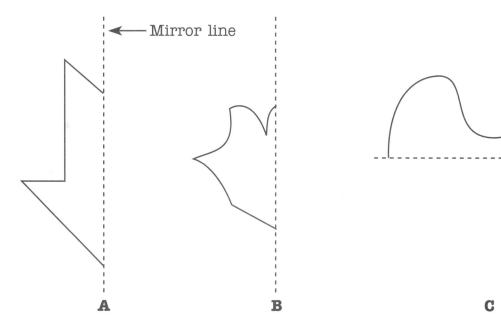

A   B   C

- -

Ms. DeCosta walked on the treadmill for 45 minutes.

She set the speed of the treadmill at 4 miles per hour.

About how many miles did she walk?

A square has 4 lines of symmetry.

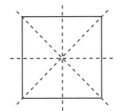

How many lines of symmetry does each figure below have?

Draw them all.

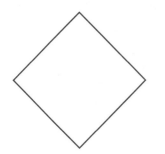 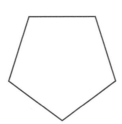 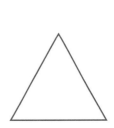 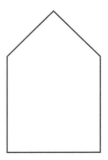

What is the mass of Box A?

- Box A and Box B have the same mass.

- Box C is 5 kilograms more than the total mass of Boxes A and B.

- Box D is 12 kilograms more than Box C.

- Box D has a mass of 39 kilograms.

 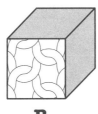  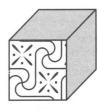

A   B   C   D

Fill in numbers so that the story makes sense.

You cut out a square.

It has _____ sides and _____ vertices.

The length of each side is _____ centimeters.

The perimeter is _____ centimeters.

The area is _____ square centimeters.

Each of the angles measures _____ degrees.

Imagine that you took 1000 giant steps.

How far from your desk could you walk?

How long would it take you to get there?

Conduct some experiments to help you answer the questions.

Make a scale drawing of the garden.

- The garden is 10 feet long and 2 feet wide.

- Each vegetable area is 2 feet wide.

- Tomatoes are on the left and take 6 square feet of the garden.

- Potatoes are on the right and take 10 square feet of the garden.

- Carrots are planted in the space that is left in the middle.

What is the area for carrots?

71

Let 1 inch = 1 foot

72

Use graph paper and block letters.

Write your first name.

Tell how many lines of symmetry each letter has.

Mr. Trout bought 3 pounds of fish for $14.37.

Ms. Flounder bought 4 pounds 8 ounces of fish for $21.24.

If the type of fish is the same, who got the better buy?

Mark made a garden 10 feet long and 3 feet wide.

He has 8 yards of garden fence.

Does he have enough fence to enclose the garden on all four sides?

Explain.

75

Estimate.

How many cups of liquid do you drink in a day?

Use that number and a calculator to estimate the number of quarts of liquid you drink in a year.

76

Chris has a rectangular-shaped sandpit.

The area of the pit is 90 square feet.

Its length and width are whole numbers.

What is the greatest perimeter possible?

What is the least perimeter possible?

Molly, Yoko, Margaret, and Rico each drew a polygon.

- Rico's polygon has no acute angles.

- Molly's polygon is a quadrilateral.

- Margaret's polygon has two sets of parallel sides.

- Yoko's polygon has a 90° angle.

Who drew each one?

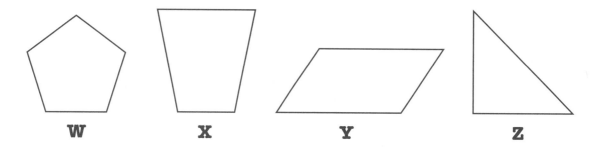

W   **X**   **Y**   **Z**

These shapes can be folded to make number cubes.

When folded, which two cubes will have the same face opposite face 1?

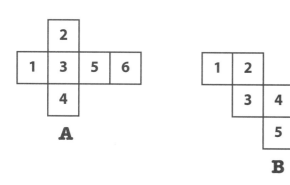

A

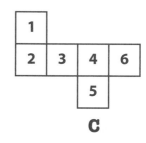

B

C

Wrapping paper was glued on to cover the 6 faces of this cube-shaped box.

How many square inches of wrapping paper were used?

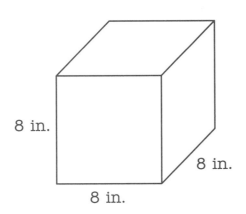

8 in.

8 in.

8 in.

Measure your height in straws.

Measure your height in large paper clips.

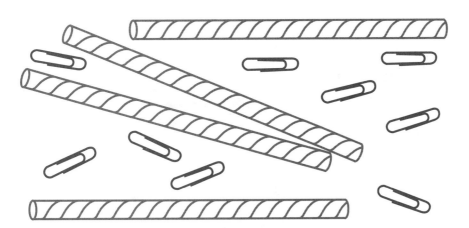

Suppose you know a person's height in straws.

How could you find that person's height in paper clips without doing any measuring?

Square Corner and Circle City are two cities between Hexagon Hills and Triangle Town on Highway 104.

- Hexagon Hills is 18 miles west of Triangle Town.

- Square Corner is 4 miles from Hexagon Hills.

- Circle City is 6 miles east of Square Corner.

Use a scale of 1 inch to represent 4 miles.

Locate the 4 cities on Highway 104.

Record the distances in miles between cities.

West   Highway 104   East

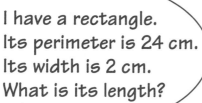

I have a rectangle.
Its perimeter is 24 cm.
Its width is 2 cm.
What is its length?

Suppose a friend asks, "What does the word *congruent* mean?"

Use words and pictures to help your friend understand.

Suppose you have 20 squares, each measuring 1 inch on a side.

Using all the squares, how many different rectangles can you construct?

What are their dimensions?

Which rectangle has the greatest perimeter?

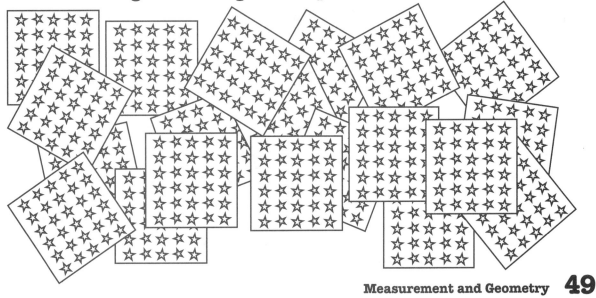

The puzzle pieces can be put together to form a large triangle.

Trace and cut out the pieces.

Fit them on the large triangle.

Draw lines on the large triangle to show how the pieces fit.

85

Puzzle Pieces

- -

Use dot paper.

Draw three different polygons, each with an area of 2 square units.

Vertices must be on the dots.

Compare your polygons with those of a classmate.

86

 = 1 square unit

Place a mirror upright on the design card.

Which of the pictures below can you make?

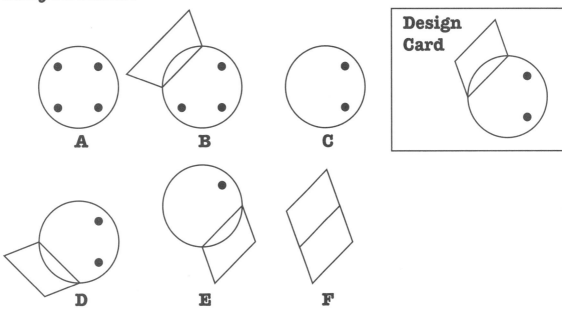

A   B   C

Design Card

D   E   F

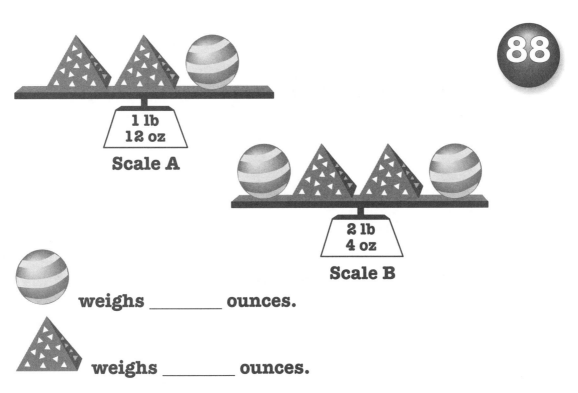

Scale A

1 lb
12 oz

Scale B

2 lb
4 oz

weighs _____ ounces.

weighs _____ ounces.

Describe the steps you used to find the weights.

This building is made with 18 blocks.

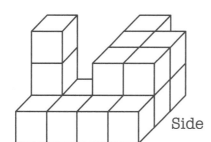

Side

Front

Shade the grids to show the top and side views.

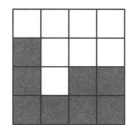

Front view

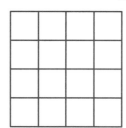

Top view

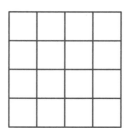

Side view

- -

Get a tangram set, or trace and cut out this tangram pattern.

If the area of the small square is 1 square unit, what is the area of

- one of the small triangles? _____

- one of the parallelograms? _____

- one of the large triangles? _____

- one of the whole patterns? _____

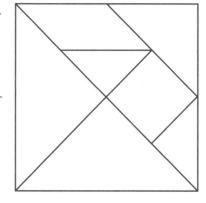

Whose school is the oldest?

Whose school is the newest?

"My school is 2 decades old."

"My school is half a century old."

"My school is 35 years old."

Lyn

Kelly

Shondra

On the graph, the ordered pair for Point *A* is (2, 5).

Draw a picture on graph paper.

Give directions to a classmate to draw your picture.

Use ordered pairs in your directions.

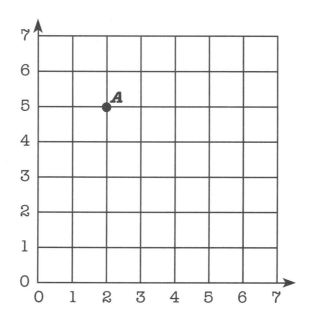

The length of a rectangle is 4 centimeters longer than its width.

The perimeter of the rectangle is 16 centimeters.

What is the length of the rectangle?

What is the width of the rectangle?

- -

Draw a triangle, a rectangle, and a square that satisfy the rules.

Rules

- The rectangle's area is 3 times the triangle's area.

- The square's perimeter is 2 times the rectangle's perimeter.

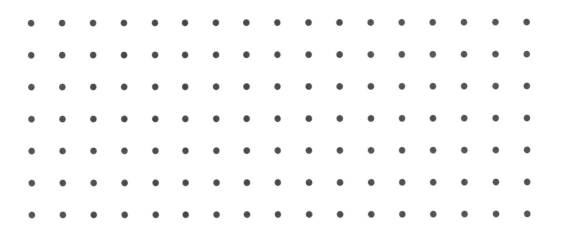

The Plumes started their drive from Beaktown to Chirpton with a full tank of gasoline.

A full tank holds 25 gallons of gas.

They used 10 gallons of gas to travel from Beaktown to Wing City.

Do they have enough gas left to make it to Chirpton?

Tell how you decided.

Route 66 North
Beaktown   50 miles
Wing City 300 miles
Chirpton   600 miles

Jeremy folded an $8\frac{1}{2}$ inch by 11 inch sheet of paper.

First he folded here.   Then he folded here.

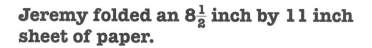

Fold lines

He cut out shapes from the folded sheet.

When he unfolded it, he saw this design:

On the folded sheet, draw the shapes that Jeremy cut.

Now make your cuts on a folded sheet of paper.

Is your design like Jeremy's?

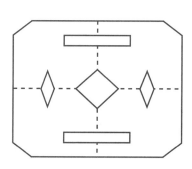

"I'm not the tallest. I weigh more than Alex."

"I don't weigh the least."

"I don't weigh the most. I am shorter than Tanya."

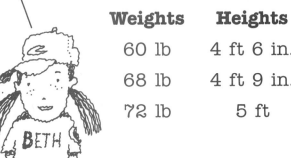

Weights	Heights
60 lb	4 ft 6 in.
68 lb	4 ft 9 in.
72 lb	5 ft

Beth weighs _____ and is _____ tall.

Tanya weighs _____ and is _____ tall.

Alex weighs _____ and is _____ tall.

- -

Assume there are no cubes you can't see, unless they are needed to hold up another cube.

What is the least number of cubes you could add to this shape to make a rectangular prism?

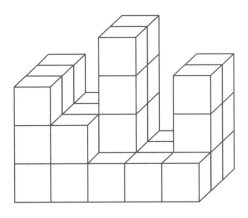

If each cube has a volume of 2 cubic units, what is the volume of the completed prism?

Patricia made a scale drawing of a sailboat.

In her scale drawing, 1 inch stands for 20 feet.

What is the actual length of the boat?

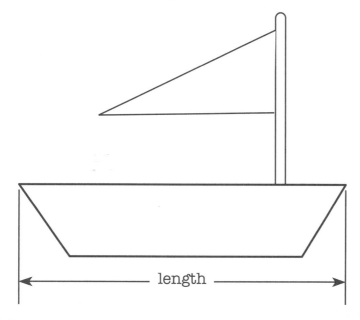

length

Get some cubes.

Make a building to match these views.

Draw a picture of your building.

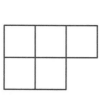

Top view

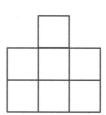

Front view

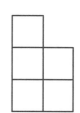

Side view

Answers

1.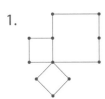

2. 2 cups, or 1 pint

3. Clue must specify position of Pedro, who is shorter than Erik. Order will be Huang, Pedro, Carl, Erik *or* Huang, Carl, Pedro, Erik *or* Pedro, Huang, Carl, Erik.

4. Answers will vary.

5. Problems will vary.

6. A, Gina; B, Kiran; C, Kyle

7. Answers should follow this form: a, 10 A.M., b, $a + b$, 1, where $a + b < 73$.

8. A, D

9. W

10. triangles: a, b, c, d; quadrilaterals: ac, cd, acd, bc; total score: 28 points

11. Answers will vary.

12. years, miles (or kilometers), feet, inches, inches, ounces

13. 5040 g

14. 2 m

15. A, D; They are 5-sided polygons with a black square at one vertex and a curve at another.

16. 2

17.

18. 4200 times

19. 66, −3, 34, 35

20. The second line is about 3 times the length of the first, or $3 \times 3 = 9$ cm, which is 90 mm.

21. triangular prism

22. Answers will vary.

23. Dells, Saks, Rose, Picó

24. 7 ways

Quarts	Pints	Cups
3	2	
3	1	2
3		4
2	4	
2	3	2
2	2	4
1	4	4

25. Possible answer: Count squares and half-squares: $4 + \frac{1}{2} + \frac{1}{2} + \frac{1}{2} = 5\frac{1}{2}$ sq units. Or, enclose the polygon in a 3-by-3 square and subtract the parts not in the square: $9 - 2 - \frac{1}{2} - \frac{1}{2} - \frac{1}{2} = 5\frac{1}{2}$ sq units.

26. Answers will vary.

27. Possible answer: A has faces that are all rectangles. B is the only solid with 5 faces. C has faces that are all triangles. D has 1 face that is curved.

28. Answers will vary.

29. 1 lb for $6.99; Possible explanation: 16 oz, or 1 lb, of the other box would be $2 \times \$3.99 = \$7.98$.

30. Possible list: 1. A rectangle has all right angles and 2 sets of parallel sides. 2. A parallelogram has 2 sets of parallel sides and opposite angles that are equal. 3. A rhombus has 4 equal sides and 2 sets of parallel sides. 4. A square has 4 equal sides and 4 right angles.

31. $7.00

32. about 5 mi or 6 mi high

33. meters, grams, liters, centimeters, kilograms

34. Lists will vary.

35. hexagon; Possible explanation: It has more sides than a pentagon, and if all the sides of the 2 figures are the same length, the figure with more sides has the greater perimeter.

36. Yes; 2 L is about 8 glasses. No; a bill has a mass of about 1 g, and he wouldn't be paid $1000. Other claims will vary.

37. 5 lb

38. the 1 lb 8 oz size; Possible explanation: 1 lb 8 oz = 24 oz, and 24 oz is twice 12 oz, and 2 × $1.80 = $3.60, which is more than $3.10.

39. 6 different prisms: 1 by 1 by 24, 1 by 2 by 12, 1 by 3 by 8, 1 by 4 by 6, 2 by 2 by 6, 2 by 3 by 4

40. D; Possible explanation: A holds 6 pt, or 3 qt; B holds 24 oz, which is less than 2 qt; C holds $\frac{1}{2}$ gal, or 2 qt; D holds 5 qt.

41. 3 rectangles (not including the square); The square's perimeter is 16 cm. Rectangles with the same perimeter are, in centimeters, 1 by 7, 2 by 6, and 3 by 5.

42. Possible answer: Boston, New York, Seattle, Miami, Phoenix; Explanations will vary.

43. 15 lb; Possible explanation: 90 is half of 180, and 15 is half of 30.

44. C

45. Take Hwy 105, drive 110 mi to Carver, turn onto Hwy 77 and drive 80 mi to Benton, and then turn onto Hwy 50 and drive 63 mi to Lyle.

46. Answers will vary.

47. 2 in.^{2}

48. 126 min; Possible explanation: 9 A.M. to 10 A.M. is 60 min, plus 6 min for each of the 11 other hours (for example, 1:09, 1:19, 1:29, 1:39, 1:49, 1:59)

49. 50 g; Possible explanation: 4 ▯ are 76 g, so 2 ▯ are 38 g; and 6 ◉ are 36 g, so 2 ◉ are 12 g; and 38 + 12 = 50 g.

50. 7 pairs; triangle and heptagon, triangle and hexagon, triangle and pentagon, quadrilateral and pentagon, quadrilateral and hexagon, 2 quadrilaterals, 2 pentagons

51. Answers will vary.

52. 36, 25, 11, 44, 175

53. Lines will vary. The figure's area is 46 no matter how the lines are drawn.

54. Answers will vary.

55. B, C, D

56. 18 more

57. five 12-oz weights, two 8-oz weights, one 4-oz weight

58. The square; since the area of the square is 49 ft^2, each side measures 7 ft, giving a perimeter of 28 ft. The rectangle is 6 ft by 4 ft, with a perimeter of 20 ft.

59. Shapes will vary.

60. $400

61. The width and height increase by 1 unit each time; 40 cubic units.

62. Isaac, Reva, Carmen, Ken, Tracy *or* Ken, Carmen, Reva, Isaac, Tracy

63. 218 more cubes

64. Arrangements will vary.

65.

A   B   C

66. 3 mi

67. 4   5   3   1

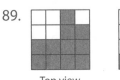

68. 11 kg

69. Answers should follow this form: 4, 4, n, $4n$, n^2, 90, where $n > 0$.

70. Answers will vary.

71.   The carrot area is 4 ft^2.

72. Answers will vary.

73. Ms. Flounder

74. No; the perimeter of the garden is 26 ft, and 8 yd is only 24 ft.

75. Totals will vary but will equal $\frac{\text{cups}}{\text{day}} \times 365 \div 4$.

76. 182 ft, 38 ft

77. W, Rico; X, Molly; Y, Margaret; Z, Yoko

78. A, C

79. 384 in.^{2}

80. Answers will vary.

81.

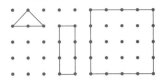

82. 10 cm

83. Answers will vary.

84. 3 rectangles; in inches, 1 by 20, 2 by 10, and 4 by 5; The 1 by 20 has the greatest perimeter.

85.

86. Some possible polygons:

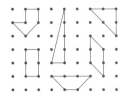

87. A, B, C

88. 8, 10; Possible explanation: The difference between the scales is 8 oz, which is due to the extra 🟤 on scale B, so the 🟤 weighs 8 oz. On scale A, the 2 🔺 must weigh 20 oz, so 1 🔺 weighs 10 oz.

89.

Top view   Side view

90. $\frac{1}{2}$ sq unit, 1 sq unit, 2 sq units, 8 sq units

91. Kelly's (50 years), Lyn's (20 years)

92. Answers will vary.

93. 6 cm, 2 cm

94. Possible answer:

95. Yes; they went 350 − 50 = 250 mi on 10 gal, an average of 25 mpg. The remaining distance is 600 − 300 = 300 mi. With 25 − 10 = 15 gal left, they can go an additional 25 × 15 = 375 mi.

96. Only one design is possible:

97. 60 lb, 4 ft 6 in.; 72 lb, 4 ft 9 in.; 68 lb, 5 ft

98. 26 cubes, 120 cubic units

99. 70 ft

100. Buildings will vary.